Toward a Unified Theory of Self

Poems

Kat Bodrie

Second Edition

brambleonline.com

Toward a Unified Theory of Self: Poems
Second Edition
by Kat Bodrie

Cover Art: Michele Rousseau
Cover Design: Kat Bodrie
Editor: Kat Bodrie
Assistant Editor: George T. Wilkerson

ISBN: 979-8-9993768-0-0

*For everyone who has helped me
toward my unified theory of self,
especially Kyndal, David,
Ryan, and George.*

I love you. I'm grateful for you.

Contents

Recipe for Oatmeal

Take an uninterrupted
morning, your favorite
newspaper. Add dry
oatmeal to boiling water
and stir. Keep stirring.
Turn down the radio
to hear the sound
of something else
roiling, fattened flakes
turning in the current,
the way they don't complain.

Genesis

She didn't want to be
the bones of her own making —
carving the rib from Adam
while he's snoring, sewing
perfect sutures that God will find later —
but He's gone, and Adam,
made in His image,
cannot be trusted.

She plucks jars from cabinets,
chicken bones from the ice box, conjures
eyes, teeth, the intractable cunt
from which sprung two sons and desire
for a daughter to whom she can teach
the only magic she knows.

Endurance

I.

Even in a happy second marriage,
there are things they must endure
of one another: his Brillo pad
laugh, her emotional drinking.
Still, it's nothing like before: the mad man
stalking into the house, raving
drunk, dropping onto bed
until work at sunrise.

Maybe she knew her fate:
he arrived late to the labor and stayed
a few minutes, enough
to glimpse the wrinkled head, fingers
flexing, reaching
for him to return.

II.

There's a first for everything
in a family. Her parents invited her
home and she worked at the bank,
saved money to move, just her
and the blonde-haired angel.
Watching the tiny chest rise and fall,
curls splayed on the pillow,
she thanked their lucky stars, whispered
There are a million things you can do
with this life.

Eyelids fluttered as she turned,
child's breath sweet,
smiling even in sleep
as if she knew that their trouble,
the hulking bulk of it,
was behind them.

III.

He was a quiet, smiling man
who lived one street over.

When she saw him
pull into the driveway
in his Toyota pickup,
she must've felt her life
teetering toward good, his simple *hi*
all the momentum she needed
to walk downhill, baby in stroller
and him alongside, to put water
on the stove and when it
started boiling, roiling in its stead,
the whistling echoed down the hall,
up the stairs, to the bedroom
where she fell upon
her future.

Betrayal

After the puffy lettering
on my Dixie Stampede t-shirt
twisted to the contours
of new breasts, I sat
across from my father
in an Applebee's booth
with his second wife, whom
he fucked while I was still nursing.
He ordered fried mozzarella
and before the sticks cooled
he gulped his share faster
than I could.

Mom made pancakes on Saturdays,
poured water from the tap
into powdery mix, margarine-fried
till bubbles broke placid tops.
I'd eat four in five bites,
pride myself on efficiency.

Entrees arrived.
He gorged on a small mountain
of oily noodles as I gnawed my sandwich, staring.
How many of my appetites were his?
How long before I betrayed
my best intentions?

Grit

I learned to let go
in fifth grade gym class,
when Rhonda Tilley said she'd
push me on a scooter.
After our teammates
crossed the finish line, I plopped
my narrow bottom on the Day-Glo seat,
fingers gripping handles
as Rhonda pushed my shoulders, ran
on skinny legs to the cone,
rounded it.

Our team was a straight shot, cheering,
and the speed made me panic.
I pressed fingertips to floor
and Rhonda's hands
shoved me forward, front teeth
exploding like fireworks.

My tongue explored the arch,
fingers picked out grit, which
I cupped in my palm until the classroom
where I decided maybe the dentist didn't need
my teeth even though they hadn't been babies.
I rubbed the grit between
my fingers like sand, letting it fall
until there was nothing left.

Rollerblading

I.

Sometimes, I go rollerblading
in my old middle school

in my mind, up the smooth ramp
that leads from the band room

past the art and computer rooms,
to sixth grade classrooms

where I learned about Russia
and space exploration

and ignored the boy I liked
because I was afraid,

but nowhere else
because the stairs

to the seventh grade
classrooms are steep,

and I don't want
to risk it.

II.

At the skating rink
the lights clicked off

and the overweight girl
who took our money

said on the intercom,
"Couples only, no kids."

Boyz II Men's "I'll Make Love to You"
played, our favorite song,

so I pulled my sister or a friend
with me because I didn't want

to stop. But sometimes
I watched watery faces

under roaming lights,
smiling, fingers locked,

and I wondered
who'd I end up with

and why
someday.

Pat

I. Elementary

She drew in pencil with a thick line
Arabian horses on recycled notebook paper

for me. They shared her buckteeth, stringy
hair. In my yearbook, I drew googly eyes

over hers, penned words in a speech bubble:
"I love horsies!"

II. Middle

In algebra for smart kids, we had a friend
whose favorite song was "Only Happy When It Rains."

We claimed it was our favorite, too.
She stopped drawing horses,

or, at least, giving them to me.
At her birthday sleepover,

I stole the silver nail polish
everyone liked, put it in my suitcase

when they were upstairs.
When someone asked if I had it,

I said no, unflinching,
but by the barn, she layered

saddle over folded blanket, strapped buckle
under bulging stomach, and I felt the knot

in my gut, too scared to ride.
In her bedroom, I fingered

countless blue ribbons, the satin
smooth on the circle, stiff on the tails.

III. High

We dug toes into cigarette sand,
stood like statues staring obsessively

at the rising sun, our desired fates:
she wanted to write in Chicago,

land of bootlegs and gangsters.
I wanted to write, too, but with

more stability and less immorality.
When we went swimming

with a male friend, the mud squishing
between our toes like Jell-O pudding,

we removed our underwear underwater
just to say we had done it. She hung

her head out the window home, said,
"Mom'll kill me if she sees my hair wet."

I heard her parents held her hostage
when she decided on college.

They'd give her a Lexus, pay tuition
to go to law school, but she wanted to go

anywhere else. I spied her on Facebook,
a law school grad. I wonder

if she's still writing or riding,
still has it down pat.

Love Like Mangos

Love is simple
like mangos at market

ripening beneath
uncertain fingers.

Epistemology

"When did you last want to leave?"

I thought I knew the answer
it's been a long time
but then it all goes back to

epistemology (n.)
how we know
what we know

a word I encountered before college
graduation like the stranger I met
asking me the question

before leaping into the unknown
of my life without school,
trying to feel out the depths

of he who challenges me daily
to see what I know and to question it.
How do I know what I know

when what I feel changes
rapidly? How do I know even
that I love him or he me?

Do some truths stay
still? Or do they swim around
like minnows we try to grasp

below surface, scales sliding
out of reach, tails whipping water
into froth?

The answer is *last week.*
The answer is *all the time.*

Rockstar

"I'm ready," I said. It was a proposition
presented like the fatty thigh
I'd draped across his
while watching *Grindhouse*.

We sat on the steps
of my sun-smothered porch
as he sucked on a cigarette.
"Now?" he said.

It didn't work.
It lay on his inner thigh.
A month before, I'd felt a fire in my belly
hearing his drawling blues, watching
bony fingers strum a split second slower
than the driving line.
He bought me a drink because the bartender
didn't ID anybody. We sat in velvet armchairs.
A stranger asked how long
we'd been together.
"We aren't dating," I said.
"I have a boyfriend back home."

In his burgundy Buick, he rolled down the window
because his parents didn't know he smoked.
At their house that night, I spied
the underside of a shelf lined
with cartoon action figures. He reached
for a tissue, and I wondered if his parents
had heard us from downstairs.

The Blue Vase

This is the blue vase from Mexico
that your mother gave me

after I told her I liked hers.
Cornflower-blue glaze drips,

hard like wedding cake
icing over a midnight

background, catching
the lamp's shine.

As you toppled the bookcase
I held it in my mind

like I do now, fingers
firmly at lip and bottom

as if our house were a museum
and every cheap thing in it

an artifact of our love
carefully preserved and positioned.

It was the reason I cried
for you to stop: if you broke it

you were liable to break anything,
even me.

Beam

We live in light
again, after nine years
in the musty apartment
whose sun never reached
the yearbooks, the back
of the kitchen cabinets.

Now, our cat demands
to look out every window
and feed at 5 a.m.
but we love her.

You lost her in the yard
last night, the weightless
corridor of flashlight beam
offering no apologies, over
and over. I saw you from
the next street over standing
on the deck, looking across the yard
at my beam skating through the trees
into the neighbor's backyard.

When I Go

I want my death to feel
like being tucked in

to bed, Pink Blankie
under one arm, thumb

cradled between my lips.

Visiting My Alma Mater

I am a ghost to this life.
I carved memories into my hands
and read them as I wander the halls—
Hawthorne and Lindsay, lines
from The Classics and my instructors
telling us consider diction and syntax,
line breaks and love.

Life has made me mellow,
like a dog. I once walked the halls
with purpose, to the library
to sell socialist newspapers
and paint a fist on the rock in red.
I kneel before this monolith
that has a life of its own now, without me.

The meditation room is still
after the door whooshes, sucking
at the hinges like a hospital's.
I sit on the floor cross-legged,
the church bell chiming, beckoning me
remember who I am, what I was,
what I heard ten years ago:
This is the time.

What choice have I
except to accept
these changes?

What tendency
but to forget?

Toward a Unified Theory of Self

I. Circle

Grocery carts
lined at registers
like O's on blood cells backstroking
down rivers in single-file lines,
cars in two neat rows
then brake lights jamming
passage, absence
of iron, the banging
of small mallets
inside
the skull.

II. Cube

The functioning of the mind
in an increasingly small space;
the sterilized, fluorescence
hall, scuff marks from chairs
dragged, heavy work boots,
and rubberized heels—
I am alone here, we are all
units in tiny packages,
dissolute in private places.

III. Cylinder

The sink-into-able couch
at my parents' house, pin pricks
of light from the tree.

Limp puppy in lap, bottle of Belg
on my mouth. I could sleep
all night right here.

IV. Rectangle

Muscles restrict, retract into
leaping refractions; I could settle
for silence, but prefer
the shaking of the mattress

and breathing out my mouth
in jagged cries: no more, more.

V. Pyramid

Mountaintop,
a man-made pile
of rocks grouted, marking
the highest spot. Ocean floods
shore in frequent storms. Cups of tea
in the warm, dry room. I would rather kneel
on damp sand, follow the gull's wayward path.

Shake Apart

Mom sets her tea
onto the patio table,
ice in cup clinking.
I've seen those shakes
in my Nan, whose cursive
handwriting jumps across
the page like she wrote
in a car driving over gravel. "How long
have they done that?" I ask.
"A few years," Mom says.
"It's getting worse."

We kiss goodbye. I climb
onto the homebound bus,
pay my fare. New passengers
eye each other nervously, glance
at the vibrating ceiling penitently.
I wonder whether the pieces
that quake with each asphaltic jolt
will shake apart any second
or hold together long enough
to carry us home.

After Close Study

Emerging from the ink-filled
womb, my bloodshot eyes

wonder at the hand
manipulating my Saturn's

gear shift, surprised physics
is a friend. I stop

at the German deli
for Schinkenbrot,

toss the loaf onto passenger seat
as if into the basket

of a Parisian bicycle
that I pedal home, where

on the porch with a glass
of cold Riesling, my husband recites

Mary Oliver aloud,
at my demand,

a reasonable extension
to soft thoughts

sliced
thin.

A Found Thing

I found a Thing on the floor today.
It's silver, metal, round,
with a hole in the side
where it screws
onto something.
It likes to roll around
the creases of my hand.
Maybe it's vital to the bed frame
and I'll be jostled awake
during a dream where I win
the lottery and revisit Europe
but can't because my head has rammed
the headboard since this Thing decided
to unscrew itself. I'll yell and scream
and it will stare up at me
like a puppy that's been bad.
Its surface will glimmer
as if to say, I didn't mean
to make you mad. I just wanted
some company.
I'll feel sorry, apologize,
tell it it can stay, that I
know how it feels
to be far away from home,
lost and alone.

Nan Watches Birds

Nan watches birds
out the bay window

snatch seeds
from the feeder,

transport them
to gaping mouths

and wait until
the quiet to eat.

Acknowledgments

A few of these poems were first published elsewhere:

“After Close Study,” *Slim Volume: This Body I Live in*
“A Found Thing,” *Baby Lawn Weekly*
“Love Like Mangos,” Poetry in Plain Sight
“Recipe for Oatmeal,” *West Texas Literary Review*

I owe a great deal to my Winston-Salem Writers prose critique group, The Yarn Spinners: Colleen Betts, Cyndi Briggs, R. Caresse Hightower, Sylvia Laurence, and Vanessa Smith. Thank you for giving me feedback on some of these poems, though poetry was not your preferred genre.

I also received helpful feedback from Mark Fleming, John Haugh, and Ellen Summer.

Thank you to my sister, Michele Rousseau, who took my rough sketch and gave it life through her brushes and artistic instincts.

I’ve developed my craft over the years with the help of many people, workshops, and programs, including the North Carolina Writers’ Network and Winston-Salem Writers. Two of my undergraduate instructors laid the groundwork for me to develop my aesthetic: Terry Kennedy and Drew Perry.

Several individuals have helped me believe in myself and my work, which led me to release the second edition of this book. Thank you to Ryan Barnard, David Johnson, Andrew Ramseur, Sam Reed, David Thomas, and George T. Wilkerson. You have my gratitude forever.

About the Cover Art

Migraines are a bitch. Mine, with aura, begin with a spotlight in the middle of my vision, which is alarming in itself, but then I become unable to use and understand language. When I first experienced this in eighth grade, it was difficult to remember and convey my home phone number to the administrative assistant in the principal's office.

Finally, a severe headache sets in, along with a sensitivity to light. I'm debilitated. I have to close the curtains and lie down or, if I can't escape the sun or fluorescent lights, pull a sweatshirt or coat over my head.

I've had a few of these occurrences — enough to analyze and somewhat take control of the process. Now, I can force myself to say things like "I have a migraine," "I don't understand," or "I need to lie down."

In summer 2017, a migraine was triggered by the bright sun reflecting on railings and windows at the community college where I worked. As I sat in my office with the light off, I saw a kaleidoscope of shifting geometric shapes against a black background. It was like a private laser light show, the only time I've ever experienced this. It was beautiful and awe-inspiring.

This experience inspired the cover design of this chapbook. My life is not as perfect or symmetrical as I'd like for it to be. The pattern is perfectly laid, but sometimes the people I meet and desires I have don't readily fit into it.

The design explodes, spilling out pieces of itself. Eventually, the gravity of some situation or state of mind slowly pulls it back in.

Writing makes the jumbled, imperfect pattern less intimidating and more like something I can love.

About the Poet

Kat Bodrie is a poet, writer and freelance editor in Winston-Salem, North Carolina. She is Book Editor for BleakHouse Publishing, co-editor of the online poetry lit mag *bramble*, and past president of Winston-Salem Writers. Along with George T. Wilkerson, who lives on death row, she is co-author of *Bone Orchard: Reflections on Life under Sentence of Death* (second edition) and *Digging Deep: Writing for Self-Discovery, Healing, & Transformation*. Kat's poems have been published in *Poetry South*, *North Meridian Review*, *Rat's Ass Review*, and more. Four of her poems have been displayed across North Carolina for Poetry in Plain Sight. Her poem "Injections," which compares pet euthanasia to death row prisoner euthanasia, was a finalist in North Carolina Poetry Society's Poet Laureate Contest. Her poetry chapbook *When the River Takes Us* was a finalist in Black Mountain Press's quarterly chapbook contest. Her ekphrastic poems "Distance" and "Resist" were featured in Charlotte Writers' Club - North's *Beyond Poems and Paintings* exhibit at Mooresville Arts. Kat was a featured poet for Sawtooth School of Visual Art's "Good Impressions: Poetry at the Pressbed" program. Her play *Sacrifice* was produced by Stained Glass Playhouse for the 10-Minute Windows Virtual Play Festival.

Kat has her Master of Arts in English literature from UNC-Wilmington and Bachelor of Arts in English from UNC Greensboro, through which she participated in the honors abroad program in London and Hull, England. In addition to writing and publishing her own poetry, she gives feedback to incarcerated individuals on their prose and poetry. She supports human rights, prisoners' rights, criminal justice reform, therapeutic resources for prisoners, and restorative justice. *katbodrie.com*

www.ingramcontent.com/pod-product-compliance
Lightning Source LLC
LaVergne TN
LVHW010835120826
845149LV00016B/2770

* 9 7 9 8 9 9 9 3 7 6 8 0 0 *